About the Author

Marin Chan is a poet who has traveled the world in search of inspiration since his twenties. Born in south-western China, he has lived in Miami, Grenada, Shanghai, Macau, and the UAE, etc., among other places, exposing him to diverse cultures that have re-shaped his passion for writing.

He has been writing bilingual poetry and prose since childhood. His words are imbued with a sense of longing and nostalgia, evoking the bittersweet emotions that come with the passage of time and the inevitability of change. His work is characterized by a keen sense of observation, an eye for detail, and a deep appreciation for the beauty and complexity of the natural world.

His writing is sure to resonate with readers of all backgrounds and cultures, and his unique perspective on the world is sure to inspire and enlighten anyone who reads his work.

To my beloved family and the little me who always dreamed
to be a poet.

Marin Chan

US AS EAGLES

Selected Poetry Collection

AUSTIN MACAULEY PUBLISHERS™

LONDON ★ CAMBRIDGE ★ NEW YORK ★ SHARJAH

ISBN – 9789948777595 – (Paperback)
ISBN – 9789948777601 – (E-Book)

Application Number: MC-10-01-5692204
Age Classification: E

Printer Name: iPrint Global Ltd
Printer Address: Witchford, England

First Published 2024
AUSTIN MACAULEY PUBLISHERS FZE
Sharjah Publishing City
P.O Box [519201]
Sharjah, UAE
www.austinmacauley.ae
+971 655 95 202

Table of content

Little Lines of Freedom   11

Little Lines of Love   21

To Sorrow   35

Days of Hay   37

Kingdom   38

A Rose   39

Feels   40

The Tree   41

The Shade   42

A Little Man   43

Mama   44

The Open Window   45

The Moon   46

Last Life   48

O, the Pouring Rain   49

God of Wind   50

Born in Storm   51

Farmer   52

Don't Worry   53

Today   54

Heart to Mend   55

Treasure   56

Will You   57

Announcement   58

The Mercy   59

In the Rain   60

I Was Alive   61

Casual Talk   62

Chronos   63

Loneliness   64

Belong   65

Till the Day Comes   66

See the Day   67

Friend   68

The Wind   69

Calla Lily   70

I Wondered…   71

Set Off for the Sun   72

Eternity   73

Flu   74

Haiku of Seasons   75

Haiku of Tears   76

Oh, Journey   77

Us as Eagles   78

Little Lines of Freedom

MERCY

I mourned the flowers blighted by the wintry cold,
As the beauty of which hadn't been beheld.
I asked the sun, "Where was the mercy you granted?"
Answered he, "In the song of life you ever chanted."

MUSICIAN

Hark! The melody lingering in stillness —
'Tis my heart strummed with intangible strings.
Albeit I am no musician with audience,
Says the world, "In solitude you'll still rejoice!"

THE SEED

In this wasted land lies the seed we plant.
They say this desert is bound to be barren.
I close my eyes while keep my heart open,
For which I'm not the only one who's still hoping.

WANDERING

I wandered in the forest with the stars.
Sirens shattered the silence into shards,
Startled the nightingale to a sudden pause,
But I journeyed from the moon to Mars.

INNOCENCE

Heavenly heavenly joy!
When innocence shined on him,
He crooned like a little boy
Whose halo never looked dim,
For his heart was light and carefree—
Lo! The angel was him!

SONG IN ME

There's a song in my body
That I sing silently,
Sometimes I dance it over
From the floor to the ceiling.

DEAR DREAM

The road into the unknown
Carries the steps of my own.
Steadfastly, I move on and on,
Away from my childhood town.
When the time has me in fear,
Only the dream I could hold dear.
If dream was a tree,
On which I was a bird perching.
My little claws
Clung to the branch, firmly,
In spite of the tempest
That attempted to tear it apart from me.

HOPE

It glimmers at the rock bottom
Of the Dale of Despair,

And rises up to the wintry sky
Where the long night stays,
The feeble flame of which
Is driving away the bleakness—
Till it's a torrid sun in my chest.

SEASONS

The seasons change like humans do.
Winter won't stay for good, nor will you.
From summer to spring, all year around,
So will life be filled with ups and downs.
When time would lament my woe,
I shall tell him to let it go.

THRIVE

In my stance against the tempest,
I devour the rain and swallow the pain.
The wind howls to bend my limbs and trunk,
But I glare at the sky, not to yield.
For the faith I steady hold—
In that storm will we thrive.

MORNING RIDE

Merriment of a horse galloping miles,
Neglect of the time and exhausting trudge,
In the rear-view mirror I'm wearing smiles,
With flicker in the eyes and beam upon the face.
I am baptized in the morning glory,
Within heavenly joy, I no longer weary.

AGLOW

1.

Looking up to the stars,

I shall be amongst them.

Wondered I,—

For I am sparkling with radiance;

My glows

Transcend their spectrum of light.

2.

Oh you,

Perish your thought of metaphorizing me

As the sun glows!

I see my own radiance—

I am unique,

Nothing compares to my refulgence at all.

FLAME

The flame in me

Burned down my agony—

The zest for life

Lit in the lugubrious sky

Became a fire

Igniting the stars in the night.

HEART ASLEEP

'Tis the season of hibernation,

Thus awaken my heart in the time of spring.

It shall burst into bloom by then.

But for now,—

Let's keep it dormant with pain.

ARMOR

My armor has been taken off
As the night will so kiss my skin fragile.
However, I couldn't presume—
Either he'd render me a dream sweet
As a bounty of reward,
Or have my flesh ripped off
For the pain beneath would taste so good.

WETLAND

We played in the gutter,
But we found the joy of heaven;
We grew hopes in the desert,
They luxuriated like in a wetland.

JEWELRY

Confidence is my outer material;
Fortitude is what my skin's made of
Beneath which is the body of virtue.
But I'm not sheepish of shedding pearls—
The best jewelry I've ever owned.

SPRING

The breeze leaking from spring
Stealthily has my heart tremulous
In the firmament where the birds sing.
The candles lit in the wintry chill
Merrily, merrily, bounce the flame
Dancing in the wind from the window side,

Till every fiber of my heart smiles
Against the tempest of the worst time.—
O, spring awaits in a hundred miles.

CHANTEUR

Every heartbeat of mine
Composes a symphony of life—
I am a chanteur
Every second I respire.

LOVE LETTER

I smiled at my smiles;
I cried for my woes
All of my emotions and feelings,
Sorrowful or joyous—
They were the love letters I wrote
For me.

ART

The canvas of life used to be blank,
Then I adorned it with the flowers of pain.—
It became a masterpiece of art.

BLUE

When the sea sensed my blue,
He sent waves to tickle my toes.
Elated as I chased him after,
Sunset afar could hear our laughter.

GIANT

I stood on your shoulders
Where you carried me steady
So I reached for the skies,
Fetching stars—
You are the giant who makes me
Greater than a comet.

DRESS

The shabby dress never covers my wounds, nor wings.
To the firmament thus I fly, transcending cloud nine.

BASK

I bask in the solitary sun—
Spring hasn't come yet
But winter has gone.

THOUGHTS

The cloud carries tons of loads on my mind,
Transporting them to the other sky yearned for.
I might have to stay where my feet must stand,
O, but have you seen the wings of my thoughts?

SHOULD

Should I put my soul in repose?
If shouldn't, why I live on the brim of the abyss?
Should I quit watching stars in reality?
If shouldn't, why delusions present themselves to me?
Should hope stand on my path and never tremble?
If should, why it recoils when my fear does strike?

HEARTBEATS

1.

This world is full of noises,

I hear nothing but my own heartbeats.

2.

I whispered to myself:

I love this world as much as I love myself,

Even when I am all over wounded.

3.

Someday,

On my way toward the sunrise,

I will grant myself forgiveness.

Someday.

BIRTHDAY

I don't have candles to blow off,

As I don't have birthdays to celebrate anymore.

I wish time could forget my aging,—

As of the moment I am living,

My age won't matter,

My life is evergreen.

BEAUTY

In this forlorn place,

I only spot TWO beautiful things—

One is the setting sun,

The other is ME.

FREEDOM

I ran after the mountain;
I ran toward the sea;
I ran to embrace the winter in me,
Somehow I found myself in freedom
That was long lost already.

DOG

I stared at the stray dog with envious eyes,
Alas! He despised me in his pitiful sight.—
I professed myself a creature of mind,
But little importance of ego can be attached
Before the creature of freedom!

NORTH

I felt the delicate touch
Of the sun shining upon my cheek;
I sang a brisk song in the snowy dale
For a herd of cows meek.
Off the road thus I pulled over,
As I came—
From the further north before.

ROOTS

My roots will not be put down
With my wings wanting for a hover above.

NEXT TIME

If I could get up again,
Together with the sunrise tomorrow,
Let me get dressed up

Like a vagrant.
I'd play with idling clouds,
With twittering birds,—
I wander in the dust of a light-hearted world,
While I collect the best moments of freedom.

FORMS

I have so many forms of life,
Because I am insatiate with being just a human.

Little Lines of Love

DESTINATION
How long will I get to the end of the journey—
Where I will find a bower in your soul,
Resting at ease after a weary trudge.
But days in and days out,
I've been dragging my body and feet,
Holding a gleam of hope
Of reaching into your sweet dream.

ANOTHER SUNRISE
When the vapor turned to dew,
From dusk the dawn arose,
Darling, I've waited on you
For another sunrise.

LINES
1.
I haven't met you for the life of me,
But somehow
you were in my poetry—
We came across
in the midst of a stanza;
And you lingered to stay

After an unfinished comma,
2.
I write you into my lines—
It never wears me out
By reading you a thousand times.

FEATHER

My love is as light as a feather—
It could travel long miles
Wherever the wind takes further.

THIRST

The rain pours to slake the drought,
But not to quench a heart thirsty for love.

ADVENTURE

1.
O, darling, if you are willing
To adventure with me,
The initial risk you are going to take
Is to be enamored of me completely!
2.
Sport with me!
Together with your romantic tricks,
Lest my heart gets tediously rusty!

DRAMA

I pluck the petals to see if he loves me,—
Yet the truth still remains uncertain,
The death of flowers is determined.

ROSY RAIN

Velvet words tinged my dream with hues of pink,
So I showered myself in the rosy rain infinite.

MORPHEUS

Dear Morpheus, You fly me into his dream,—
And let him into mine.

FALL

I wished upon the falling stars—
Let me fall
Let me fall
Let me fall
Into that unfathomable
Depth of love.

PIPE DREAM

You were the pipe dream I hardly attain;
It became the reality replete with pain.
So aware I was, so aware I was, Entwined in the dreams,
The remnant of happiness could remain.

RENDEZ-VOUS

Rose petals, dim lights, brilliance on your face,
Rendezvous of two lonesome souls,
Casual talk, dirty jokes randomly shared,
Fierce eyes met in the subsiding sunset,
Reflections on the utensils danced with the flame
Till time and the world were left behind,
In the void of loneliness only we exist
As the rose grows a garden in the desert.

WAKE-UP

Every morning I woke up with the sun arising.
The moon must've kissed me before his departure
Without me knowing.
Because such a sweet and sound dream I was having—
Just beside him.

STAR IN EYES

1.
We were lying on the couch
Looking up at the ceilings
"Tonight the stars are sparkling"
"Not when your eyes are shining."
2.
Amongst the stars in the Milky Way,
I spot you sparkling like a diamond queen.
If tonight had the moonlight deprived,
Would you shine through the dark,
And bring me the brightest delight?
3.
"Hush, there are no words needed—
When you have dazzles in the eyes."

FROM THE MOMENT

I will hold you tight in my arms,
Taking away your agonizing tears,
Guarding you through thousands of nights.
From this moment and beyond,
I am here with you and will always be.
No woes and worry,
Will you sleep soundly like a newborn baby.

ARMS

In a storm I withstand.
But in the arms of yours—
I yield to resist.

BREEZE

We played with the wind
in the wilderness,
As the wind caressed
our bodies and skins.
I remembered your tender kiss
On my forehead, on my cheeks,
Along with every breath you took,
I felt the breeze in my lungs.

KISS

When your lips began to touch mine,
The daze had us through infinite space and time.
Then I glimpsed a world from your dazzling eyes,
where two souls were free from demise.

BEE

I tasted the sweet words
Between your honey lips—
'Tis the moment when I feel
Like I were a bee gathering nectar
From every morning flower of yours.

ELIXIR

You kissed me where I was broken—
Love is the elixir
That heals my everything.

DAYLIGHT

You brought the light
Shining through my darkest night.
But you told me you were still sorry
For not being the daytime.
Oh, darling, you must know—
You've brightened every corner of my life.

ESCAPE

Let's escape to the moon,
From the morn to the noon!
Faraway from our town,
Would no one have us found.—
When heaven does ascend,
Delight would never end!

HARBOR

I anchored myself off to your chest—
You were the harbor I called home.

CHERRY FLOWER

He who came to my garden,
Nurtured the blossom of spring.
On the wasteland it has been,
Cherry flowers he grew for me.

WASTELAND

You came like river floods
Sweeping everything away
From me pitilessly.
Till a wasteland I turned to be.

BREATH

Breathe in, breathe out,
The air you trembled conveyed to me
A lovey-dovey message
Lingering around my ears
Till which parched my body.
I barely moved myself
To the other side of the bed
That I deemed a sweet quay
Where I moored till the next morning.
Your gentle breath and loving touch
Locked me in security,
And the softness of dreams where
I was so willing to be.
I felt the air, the warmth and
Our destiny interwoven
Into another poetry.

STARDUST

In a million light years the star dies,
My love shimmers in the ruins of stardust.

LOVE IS A FLOWER

My love was a flower in the bleakness.—
Beneath the dismal ground,
It roots so deep.
It might weep in the east wind,
But never will it wither
For a single teardrop.

OCEAN

He took my tears away
From thousands of moist nights;
He never spilled after hearing
The most hideous secrets of mine;
He never loved me less
For whom I truly was.
In his eyes, forever I was that child,
On every somber night,
Who roamed along his chest line.

SLEEPLESS

The night was asleep, but I wasn't.
I drifted into the world with a sober mind
Like a homeless ghost,
Seeking and searching for a place
Where my humble being could rest,
Until I found myself curling up
In your arms, against your chest.

O, I MISSED YOU

Every second I have missed you
Has become old centuries long.
Each day I have loved you
Has the eternity to shed light on.

THE SUN

I saw your wrinkled frown
Ironed neat by the rising sun.
But later you told me,
It was me with my shining presence
That brought the darkness down—
The daybreak sun would break your dark,
But you don't know, you don't know,
She would also break your heart.

BEST TIME

He who saw the worst of me
Has stayed grasping my hand still—
It is the best of my worst time.

FOREVERNESS

The second when time stops all of a sudden,
Love becomes an eternal thing.
And you, you are the foreverness
Of my universe where the sun never sets.

REGRET

Never could I regret
Getting on board with you—
After the ocean's madness

We were embraced
In its post-storm peace—
'Twas a thrilling adventure for me.

SINK

I let myself sink
Into the ocean of loving you.
Thousands miles below the sea level,
I peek at my gravestone.

LONELY MOON

Under the moon was standing a man
With a rose bouquet drooping in hand,
Shedding the silent tears in the moonlight
As withered as the flowers, lifeless, dead.
"The heart was meant to be broken," as said,
But how wishful, his heart to be mended.
Just underneath this lonely moon.

FIASCO

The moment when you won over my heart,
My fiasco was announced—
Your triumph was my romantic defeat.

WORDLESS

Silence, we remained in silence—
The words were deprived
From the lips we used to kiss.

MELT

In my small palm I could melt the winter snow,
But I couldn't melt the icy walls between me and you.
Somehow, they said the winter was cruel.

LET RAIN

Let it mizzle,
Let it pour,
Let it flood my barren field of love.
Let the wind sweep,
Let the rain cleanse,
Let the sky clear ere the shine will re-tint.

FOR THE LAST TIME

A new journey is so well yearned,
But I wasn't ready for a farewell.
To my past—
For the last time,
Could we lie down on the beach and count the stars?
For the last time,
Could you hold me in your arms and take me to your dreams?
For the last time,
Let me away from my sorrow and frowns.
Then I will leave for tomorrow's sunrise
Without regrets and tears.

MONSOON

You were my season monsoon,
Into the river you had my heart drowned.
Till I became an island marooned,
Surrounded by the waters you have to run.

NO LONGER YOU WERE MISSED

No longer you were missed,
For the nosegay deliberate not to bloom,
Withered in the wind desperate,
Sooner or later would die in the bleak.
Although the fallen petals wished to stay,
At least to be noticed when you were in dismay.
But—
No longer you are being missed,
The mountain has turned to the plain;
The pool you swam has become an ocean,
In which every piece of you dissolves
Into nothing.
Just someday when you decided to sing again,
Would you think of the beguiled haze,
Or would you still think of me in a daze?

GAME OF LOVE

We promised not to fall in love
For whoever falls first loses—
We call it the "Game of Love."

TIPSY

Drunken stars fall into my glass of wine,
A pinch of dust glitters in the tears of mine—
Whilst the moon wanes in different forms,
Out of which he fathoms no wounds.
Sunk into the drowsy night,
I saw a dream that used to fly high—
Soaring up to the cloud nine,
But he who departed made me sigh.

RECOLLECTION

Time is fleeting
With you slipping away
From my best recollection—
Till one day,
Your presence makes no sense
To my world;
To my being.

AWAIT

He departed whence he arrived.
When the sun is down to set,
The moon will await—
But he set off for good,
While in vain I still wait.

ECLIPSE

My heart aches like a lunar eclipse,
Or much worse—
A full moon quickly it will relapse;
While fragments of the heart
Still remain unfixed pieces.

THORNS

My rose grows with thorns—
The defense mechanism
Against hurt and break.
I am rather sorry
If it does cause you to bleed.

FORGET

It took me a village to forget a fraction of you,

But all of a sudden, When a bit of the memory began to set in,

It went futile immediately.

To Sorrow

Reeling alone on the nighted street,
Toward the moon, I was up to the cliff.
The ocean was calm in his deep breath,
Mom must be building a fire in her hearth—
On the coastline road I strolled alone,
The moon was still far to reach, but I missed home.
Waves patted the rocks in constant motion,
Which reminded me of the delusion—
I was the thunder, you were the lightning,
We chased in the clouds, kissing in the rain.
When the sun came out dying the sky blue;
Where we rejoiced was covered in mildew.
The sea dazzled under the moon of autumn,
Like the marbles lost in childhood, oblivion.
As the wind sent the chills from the valley hill,
I misheard Granny's calling when I was ill—
It was the sirens lingering in the air
But somehow, my lids were wet by the tear.
On the meadow I lay with the night dew,
The grasshopper murmured, "Tomorrow would be new."

Why couldn't I be sure? Why couldn't I be sure—
What if I'd be deserted again in the moor?
Hither on the bough nigh perched a sparrow,
Replying, "It was your sorrow; it was your sorrow."

Days of Hay

Lying on the ground,
Near the construction site,
Adjacent to the outside sun,
They are napping
Away from the secular fun.
I pass by at a gentle pace,
Not wanting to make a noise.
As they must be in the dream
Where they meet their kids in gleam.
When a cloud comes above,
I pray it rains as if it could
To withdraw the scorching heat,
To nourish the abundant shade.
When the wind blows near,
I tell it to chill the air,
But don't, don't blow their dreams away,
For they're living their days of hay.

Kingdom

I used to reign the house of my parents.
My throne sat on my father's shoulders.
Everything was fairly within my reach—
O, such was my kingdom, the Kingdom of Liberty.

A Rose

39

The sunset sent the sheep home—
The shabby hut of the two
The moon returned whence it left
So she wept her heart bereft—
In that lonely stoned graveyard,
A rose was on her forever guard.

Feels

I feel the summer along the beach,
The salty air mixing with the smell of heat
From the sandy ground,
From the azure ocean.
I feel the refreshing breeze
Quaking the boughs
On which the birds are resting,
Constantly gossiping.
I feel the smoothie in your hands
With refresh pulps of fruits,
Cooling down your heat
In a mouthful you haste.
Reposing in the bower,
We pause our lives for a moment.
The sun sets in the golden hour,
Glowing with shining adornment.
I feel the life was a laid-back song
Orchestrating with the chatting crowd,
With the melody I am humming along,
And tuning with waves motion aloud.
O, life at the moment is such a song!

The Tree

I can't imagine to be a tree,
Being placed near the entrance,
Where can be seen.
I can't imagine the tree
Planted in a small pot of earth,
Suffocated to breathe.
It's the tree, a lonely tree
Who likes to play with the dust,
Sometimes with a bee.
It's the tree who loves to daydream
In the midst of the forest
Where his feet finally reach the stream.
This is the tree,
Guarding the gate like a soldier, steady,
But whose roots are confined, not free!

The Shade

Hiding myself in the shade,
I was watching the rest of the world
Getting burned in the heat.
I can't help to think of the hell,
Where the sinful would be sentenced,
Also the devils dwell.
Only the true kindness might survive
Or the ones wont to play tricks might do?
Fair or not, the shade wouldn't know,
Whose duty is not existential, never due.
Of all the virtues the shade's owned,
It comes nothing essential
But the being of itself—
a shade in the heat,
A shelter to the fretful.

A Little Man

A little man hied home,
Before the moon rose alone.
The mother was behind,
Whose cheek was rosy, divine.
They rushed in the dim sunlight,
Smiling when passing me by.
'Twas the after-school hour,
The little man regained power.
He carried the bags full
With efforts of an easy pull,
Looking back at his mom,
He waited her catching up.
When they kept up the pace,
The road lamp lit up their trace—
Sandy road they walked through,
Step by step, till they got home.
Sleep, you little man, you sleep,
Before the moon showed up at the door.

Mama

In the yard of childhood,
We lay on the meadow.
Under the mighty dome of night,
I heard Mom used to sigh.
When I counted the stars,
She was saddened by the larks;
Sometimes she would weep quiet,
But I couldn't have her tears wiped.

The Open Window

45

Tonight the window was open,
As I wished upon the stars
For the night fairy's comin'
To expel the dream eaters
And convoy me to the kingdom.
Tonight the window was open,
The moonlight wasn't very shy.
He came to my bedside quiet,
Singing me a lullaby,
Wrapping me in his pure light.
Tonight the window was open,
Many a dream would fly outside
Like, a freed bird sought for heaven,
Soared up and flew to the further sky
And became a star to glisten.
Tonight the window was open,
You guarded my sweet reign.
The fear was gone for no more,
Thus, my dream was free and secure
As, tonight, the window was so open.

The Moon

The moon discerned my sorrow,
For I roamed with my shadow.
On this long, long road I set my feet,
With nobody I fancied to meet.
So alone with my heart shut,
Lest my world got crumbled up.
The moonlight kissed me for atonement,
I closed eyes, savoring the moment.
For yonks the moon had watched me,
From the mountain to the sea,
Till my solitude became a song,
Only the nightingale cared to sing—
A tune nobody could hear
Even with a sober ear,
Thus I wailed in the lines which I wrote
Till the grief wore the gratitude's coat.
So I roamed alone with the moon,
With whom my heart was shared soon.
If the sun could detect my sorrow,
Will it mock? Or will it swallow?

I looked at the moon, frowned—
A fretful to be fondled.
But the moon was silent to respond,
With my sorrow being watched beyond.

Last Life

48

My eyes harbored the gem-blue
Of pain the sea would know,
In search of the bier below,
Where I lay my body ill
And rested my humble soul.
In the chilly wind I stood,
A face sapless in the hood,
The chill slayed as if it could.
O, assuredly it could,
Thus take me within the ash and soot.
For a life I'd been a bore,
Marrying into a heart sore,
Nobody I grew as poor,
No one stepped over my door.
If God rendered one chance more—
This time must be seized upon,
Without a grieved heart to groan.
For the sea I'd sing a song,
With my love chanting along—
Before this life will be long gone.

O, the Pouring Rain

When the world was pouring with rain,
In which I was dancing and listening
To the raindrops hitting drumbeats constantly.
On the rooftop,
On the sidewalk,
On the earthy ground…
Harmonious was such a symphony!
My bare feet were feeling the brook of rain,
Running through my toes,
Kissing my ankles intensely,
Sending a series of thrills down my spines.
I was made irresistible
To fall into the temptation of the rain.
O, the pouring rain!

God of Wind

Adrift above the clouds in the sky,
I see the moon driving the darkness out of sight,
Till the golden gauze veils the world
From side to side.
Floating in the middle of the Milky Way,
I hear a maid weeping as the tides fade away.
If I send the wind to blow her tears dry,
Would she cease to cry,
Or sleep forever in the night?

Born in Storm

51

We were born in storms,
Hearing the howling of the world—
Threat, hatred, wrath, denial…
We grew in the rains,
Stretching roots deep down in the soil,
Absorbing the nutrients,
Out of which our roots touch—
Boulders, corpses, trash…
Till we luxuriate, one day—
Confronting the sun with our
Final strength, or,
Last breath.

Farmer

52

I'm no farmer with fields to harvest.
The only thing I could reap is your tears.
After I wipe 'em off from your face,—
They are glistening like diamond grains.

Don't Worry

53

Don't worry, dear,
Let faith take you
To the day after and after—
When the night ends,
Will you see the sun eventually arises;
The light shall come to your end,
Even from a very distance.

Today

54

We laughed so hard,
When today finally put an end
To yesterday's agony.
Thus, we thought ourselves
That tomorrow ain't that far
From what we were dreaming.

Heart to Mend

55

Sunshine streams in
The life I used to throw.
As solitude started
Patching my heart that was torn—
On this unknown ground,
No one could ever mend it but you.

Treasure

56

Someday, I dreamed—
My bruises turned to golds,
Tears I burst out of my eyes
Became pearly diamonds,
And a treasure map was well hidden
In broken pieces of heart
That I concealed in a jigsaw box.

Will You

"If it rains in my world,
Could I borrow some sunlight?
Don't worry, I will give it back,
Along with an arc of the rainbow."
I asked.

Announcement

58

He who is permitted to come
To my life is supposed to make peace—
Whoever will go against it
Shall be banished out of the galaxy
Without any diadem.

The Mercy

59

What can reward the life I lead
As I've put so much effort into it?
If mercy could be granted,
Will the sun come out to applaud
After my sky is slashed by a storm?

In the Rain

Someday, on my parade
Even if it will rain,
I still will dance with you
In a whole world of rain.

I Was Alive

The reason of me being alive
wasn't the breath I took,
Or the heart I pumped.
Though my body was buried
In a corner of the graveyard
Where the Great forever slept.
Yet my soul awakened and arose
In the ash of the past,
When fire had me devoured,
Somehow I was still alive.
Alive in the world I used to live,
Alive in the oblivion
That people tended to forget…

Casual Talk

I love to keep things unsaid,
Lest I somehow jinx it.
If you know me well,
Well enough to know the unsaid,
O, trust me, I do mean it.

Chronos

63

O, Chronos,
If you could hear my heart out,
Will you let me dwell on the past
Where he forever exists.

Loneliness

64

After the ocean tide recedes,
I turn back into the deserted island.
The water used to kiss my coastline,
But now they ignore me and where I stand.
O, in this feeble moment so lonely I am.

Belong

At some point, where life has taken me
Is where my heart truly wants to belong,
Which I might not realize for the life of me.

Till the Day Comes

Before the break of dawn,
The night is always prolonged.
But the first light awaits ahead.
It's said only when you will be enough patient,
The day will eventually come.

See the Day

The dark, I saw the dark of the sea
diving for me with a multitude of massive waves and leaving
me—
A crumbled canoe scattered into pieces,
Floating on the surface of a condemned fate.
But I refused to sink,
Not yet sinking into the dark of the sea,
Even it attempted to pull me down to the abyss,
However, against the tidal force and gravity,
I made it to the day—
What the dark failed to take from me has seen the day
With the sun rising right before me.

Friend

If the whole world stands
Before me as a foe,
Will you be my friend,
Or I will be on my own?

The Wind

69

I let go of the wind I couldn't grasp,
So I pressed my lips to his forehead,
Telling him,
"I didn't expect you would stay for good,
Which you couldn't—
So I only wish you could treat me well.
Like the wind that would never turn into a gale,
Attempting to sweep down my world in its trail."

Calla Lily

I shall not compare you to the calla lily,
As the beauty of which is but a fraction of yours;
I shall not pluck the buds of blossom
As the remembrance of motherly love of eternity.
For heaven's sake, I could not help but do so—
To lay the flowers in the memory
Where your immortal presence is sorely missed!

I Wondered...

I wondered, have you ever think of me,
When the shooting stars crossed the sky where you looked up
in search of the broken wings of a leaving seabird?
I wondered, have you ever imagined me strolling beside you
again on the impalpable sands when you stared at the moon
rising above from a distance?
You must think of me, I reckoned, even if you must decide to
forget me little by little—
But little by little, you think of me when the sea passed the
message and pushed my shadows to your feet where I used to
exist.

Set Off for the Sun

72

I lost my bearings in yesterday's pain,
Somehow, I heard tomorrow's calling—
Set off for the sun; it will heal
The pain will be sealed into the past as it will.

Eternity

73

When the sun goes out,
And the stars keep falling,
We exist in the poetry of eternity.

Flu

74

I am your little flu,
Every time you cough,
I become a dazzling star.
And you,
You burst like confetti
 Forth into my heart!

Haiku of Seasons

SPRING
Spring secretly blooms
On a less-traveled road,
So does my dear dream.

SUMMER
Crickets chirp in the grass
A flowing brook choruses
Summer song repeats

AUTUMN
The wheat field ripens
Sheep bleat and the church bell echoes
He comes to harvest

WINTER
The night falls sooner
Prior to dusk the birds go south
The winter befalls.

Haiku of Tears

76

1.
The candle burns out
The dark shrouds my eyes again
I hear you sobbing.
2.
The wind blows in rage,
The waves clap hard on the cliff.
I wail in chaos.
3.
I sail in despair
But hope is the beacon
Toward which I ain't stray
4.
I soaked in the rain
The flood washed on my face—
Either tears or rain.

Oh, Journey

77

One day I told my mom,
I am gonna sail away,
Till the cows come home,
I shall return to the place
Where I left for the dawn.

Us as Eagles

When the sky is just a sky,
Stars are nowhere to shine;
When the river is just a river,
It meanders further and further;
When we are so told
That we are just beings of human,
What we forfeit is pure chance,
Without flapping the wings,
To soar, to hover.
But let us be eagles exploring the borders
Of the sky, and the ocean;
Let us be eagles,
We fly dreams and imaginations.
Never could we depart from the heavens,
When we are us as eagles.